STAINED GLASS PRIMER

the basic skills :

by
PETER MOLLICA

edited by
NORM FOGEL

photography by
CHARLES FRIZZELL

mollica stained glass press

10033 BROADWAY TERRACE, — OAKLAND, CA. 94611

To Maestro Rufo

ISBN 0-9601306-6-7

TABLE OF CONTENTS

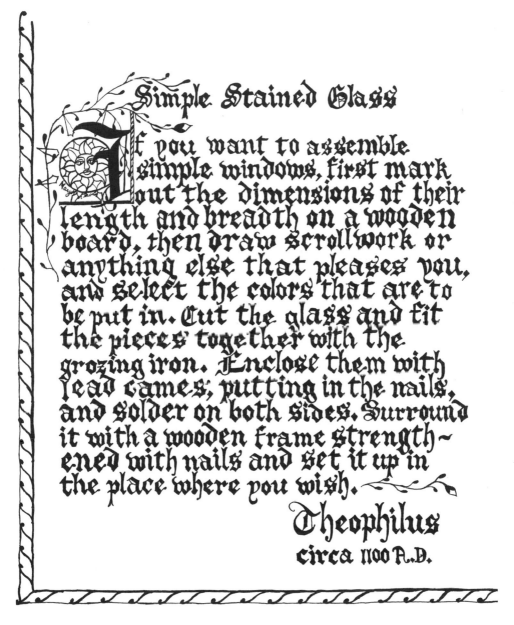

Simple Stained Glass

If you want to assemble simple windows, first mark out the dimensions of their length and breadth on a wooden board, then draw scrollwork or anything else that pleases you, and select the colors that are to be put in. Cut the glass and fit the pieces together with the grozing iron. Enclose them with lead cames, putting in the nails, and solder on both sides. Surround it with a wooden frame strengthened with nails and set it up in the place where you wish.

Theophilus
circa 1100 A.D.

Leaded Glass Panel.
Fig. 1

Introduction

The purpose of this book is to present the basics of leaded glass work. This is achieved by guiding you in making the leaded glass panel shown in Fig. 1. The full size drawing (cartoon) for the panel is inserted in the back of this book.

The techniques described and illustrated in this book are often only one of several satisfactory alternatives. Most of the alternative leaded glass techniques may be found in books listed in the bibliography of in-print stained and leaded glass books.

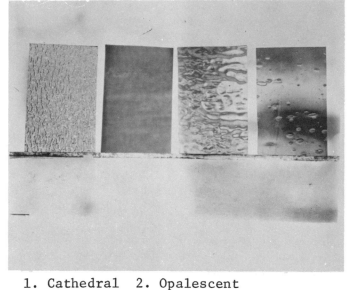

1. Cathedral   2. Opalescent
3. Blenko Antique   4. European Antique
Fig. 2

A large teardrop or cylindrical shape
blown by the glassblower is cut open
and flattened into an irregular sheet
varying in shade from front to end.
Fig. 3

Chapter 1
Glass and Glass Cutting

Any type of glass may be used in leaded windows. Some of the commonly used glasses are shown in Fig. 2.

Cathedral and Opalescent are machine made and generally available in the USA. Cathedral and Opalescent glass come in a wide variety of colors and textures. Blenko "Antique" is American hand-blown glass. European "Antique" is hand-blown glass primarily imported from England, France, and Germany.

The easiest method to locate the different types of colored glass is to look in the yellow pages for your town under "Glass, leaded & stained."

Antique glass is available in hundreds of shades of colors in sheets varying in thickness from 1/8" or thinner to 1/4" or greater. The variance in thickness results in different shades of color in the same sheet of glass (Fig. 3).

Stained glass is obtained by the addition of small quantities of various metal oxides to the purified sand from which the glass is made.

Glass cutter.
Fig. 4

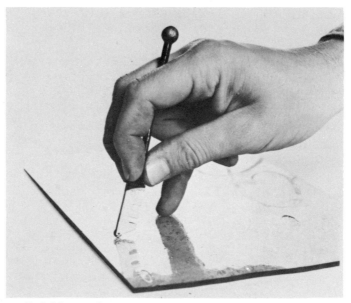

Holding glass cutter.
Fig. 5

Cutting glass requires the most practice of the basic stained glass techniques. It is a two-step process consisting of making a light scratch (score) on the surface of the glass and breaking the glass along the scored line. The best type of glass cutter for stained glass work is the Fletcher 02 or Red Devil 023 steel wheel cutter (Fig. 4).

The glass cutter, held between the index and middle fingers, is grasped with the tips of the thumb, index, and middle fingers (Fig. 5).

Before attempting to score and break scrap window glass, you will need, besides a glass cutter and scrap glass, a good flat cutting board, safety glasses, and a bench brush.

You should obtain kerosene and keep your cutter in a small can with about 1/8" of kerosene in the bottom. The kerosene cleans and lubricates the wheel. This gives a better cut and prolongs the life of the cutter.

Upsom board (pressed paper) makes a fine cutting board. A thick pad of paper plopped over with the cardboard back up is also satisfactory.

If you wear glasses then you can avoid buying safety glasses. Otherwise, purchase a pair with glass lenses. Safety glasses may be difficult to locate. Very pale sunglasses are an acceptable substitute. In any case, don't cut glass without protection for your eyes.

Scoring glass to be
broken.
Fig. 6

Breaking scored
piece of glass.
Fig. 7

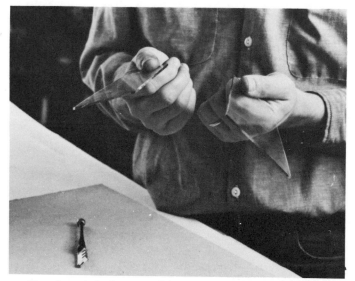

Hand positions after glass is broken.
Fig. 8

To score glass place the cutter upright about 1/8" from the far edge of the piece to be scored and, applying a firm constant pressure, draw the cutter toward you. Practice straight cuts on your scrap window glass until you know how hard to press to get an even score line. DO NOT GO OVER A SCORE. This will dull the wheel of your cutter and the score will not break correctly.

Now that you have a feel for how much pressure to apply, throw away the scored glass, brush your cutting board clean, and make a single score down the center of a fresh piece of glass, letting the cutter go off the edge closest to you (Fig. 6). If the score is clean and even, with no skips, then make a fist with each hand, grasp the glass between thumb and index finger on each side of the end of the score, and make a quick up and outward motion with your hands as though to spread your thumbs apart. The glass will crack and break along the score (Figs. 7, 8).

Now attempt cutting some gentle curves. Score and break them the same way as you did the straight cuts.

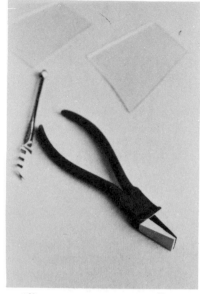

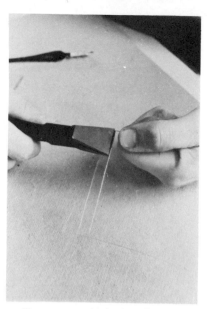

6" nippers with 1"
jaws.
Fig. 9

Proper positioning
of nippers.
Fig. 10

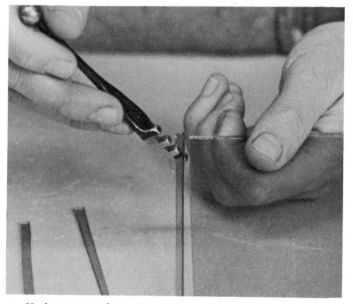

Using notches in cutter.
Fig. 11

At this point two types of pliers become useful (Fig. 9). First are nippers which come in sizes from 6" to 10" or 12" with jaw widths of 1/4" to 1". The larger nippers are for thick plate glass. You will find the 6" size to be best for leaded glass work. Nippers help break off pieces of glass too small to grasp with your hands. Place the end of the jaws parallel to the score and, being careful not to squeeze hard on the glass, use the nippers as a lever in place of one hand (Fig. 10). The movement of your hands to break glass when using nippers is the same upward and out motion as described previously.

The glass cutter has three notches (1/8", 5/32", 3/16") that are also useful in breaking off small strips of glass. Use the smallest notch that is loose on the edge of the glass and place it approximately 1/2" along the score. An outward snap will break off the strip (Fig. 11).

The other plier is called a grozier and is simply a flat nose plier with the temper removed from the metal. Groziers are used for cleaning up ragged edges of glass that don't break clean, and to aid in shaping difficult cuts. Groziers can be easily made. Buy the cheapest pair of flat nosed pliers you can find and get your local blacksmith to take the temper out of the steel. Lacking a local blacksmith, get a

Grozier being used to shape piece of glass.

Fig. 12

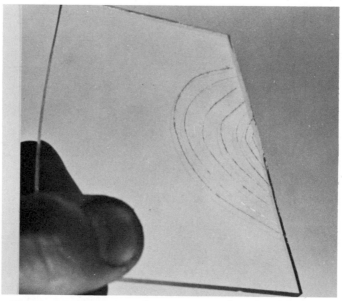

Deep curve scored to save the inside curve.

Fig. 13

Bernz-O-Matic torch, heat the plier jaws red
hot, and let them slowly cool. When soft
you will be able to round the edges of the
pliers with a file.

The action used in grozing is difficult
to describe, but it is closest to chewing
at the side of your mouth with your back
teeth. You should practice this motion on
scrap glass until you can turn out a small,
reasonably even circle (Fig. 12). Using
the edge of the jaws, grasp firmly the
chip of glass to be grozed away and
turning your wrist outward as you close
the jaws "chew" or "groze" away the
unwanted chip.

The only important cut left for you to
learn is the deep curve. This is done by
making a single score the shape that you
desire and then a series of progressive
concentric scores toward the edge of the
piece that you are going to discard. The
piece to be discarded is then broken away
in a series leading from the shallowest
curve to the deepest (Fig. 13).

You've now learned enough to cut all the
pieces for the practice panel in Fig. 1;
but before proceeding to make the panel,
one other cutting technique that will
assist you in the future will be explained.

Deep concave scores and any scores in
very thick glass can be helped to break
along the score by tapping the underside
of the score with the ball end of the
glass cutter.

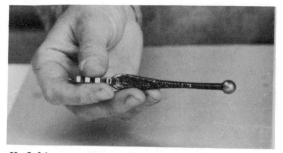

Holding cutter for tapping.
Fig. 14

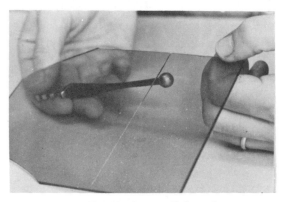

Position of hands
while tapping.
Fig. 15

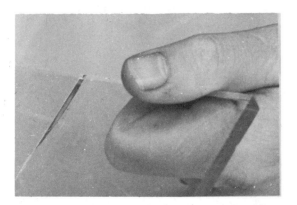

Run that appears from accurate tap.
Fig. 16

Use thumb and index fingers to hold the cutter by the end with the notches (Fig. 14). Use the middle and ring fingers to push up on the shaft and tap ONCE directly under the score and about a half inch from the end of the score (Fig. 15). An accurate tap causes a crack or "run" that appears as a dark shadow in the score (Fig. 16).

Once a run starts the break will follow the score unless there are skips in the score line. If the score line has skips in it you either are not applying enough pressure, or you have a cutter that ought to be discarded because it is chipped or has a flat spot on the wheel.

If a curve is particularly deep you may tap several times starting at one end of the curve, proceeding around the curve to the other end, or from each end in toward the deepest point of the curve, or from the middle out toward the ends. After the score has run the length of the curve, the excess may fall out or be easily pulled out. If not, make a series of scores as shown in Fig. 13 and individually break out each piece of the excess, using your nippers.

Tapping should not be used on very thin glass, less than 1/16" thick, or on strips less than 1/4" in width. The very thin glass often shatters from a tap, as will any glass from too hard a tap, and narrow strips usually don't run. A further disadvantage is that tapping leaves an irregular edge that has to be grozed.

Practice panel.
Fig. 1

Chapter 2
Cutting Glass to Shape

Your first leaded glass panel should be
designed to develop glass cutting, leading,
and soldering skills rather than to
produce a work of art.

An initial panel size of about 10" x 12"
is suggested. This allows you to work with
ten or twenty reasonable size pieces of
glass. Very small and oddly shaped pieces
of glass are difficult both to cut and
lead. They should be avoided.

The remainder of this chapter and the
next chapter are keyed to cutting and
leading this panel (Fig. 1).

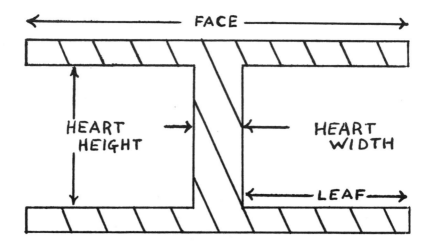

FLAT LEAD : CROSS-SECTION

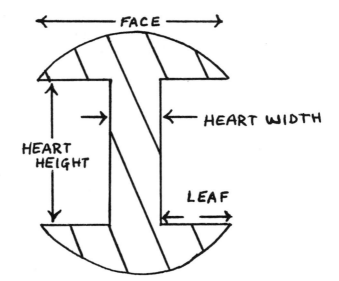

ROUND LEAD : CROSS-SECTION

FIG. 2

The next step is to make a working drawing called a cartoon. Hard surface paper such as butcher paper or kraft paper work well and are easily obtainable. Soft paper, charcoal drawing paper for example, will tear and wear during the continuous use given the cartoon.

Take a piece of cartoon paper that is 14" x 18". Next, lay out the perimeter of the panel, 10" x 12", with a 90° square; and be sure it is centered. 1/2" flat lead will be used as outside lead and 1/4" round will be used between the pieces of glass in the panel (Fig. 2).

Cross section of 1/2" flat lead
showing empty outside leaves.
Fig. 3

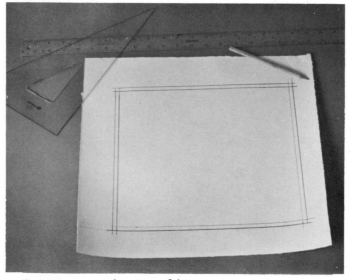

Cartoon perimeter lines.
Fig. 4

The outside leaf of the 1/2" flat lead
will remain empty (Fig. 3). To allow for
this approximately 1/4" leaf draw a second
rectangle inside the 10" x 12" perimeter
that is 1/4" from all sides of the outside
rectangle. Your cartoon should now look as
in Fig. 4. The extra width of lead
surrounding the finished panel can be
trimmed to fit the panel into a warped
window frame and is used to secure the
panel in a wood frame using carpet tacks.

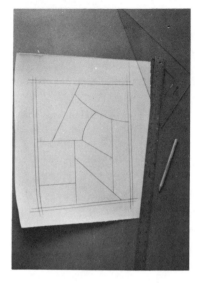

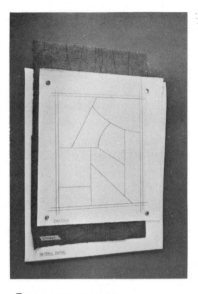

Cartoon for practice
panel.
      Fig. 5

Pattern paper,
carbon paper, and
cartoon ready to be
traced.
      Fig. 6

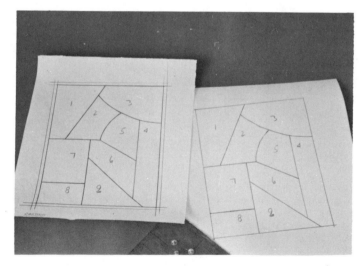

Design traced onto pattern paper and
numbered.
         Fig. 7

Draw the practice design within the inside perimeter line of your cartoon, as in Fig. 5. You are now ready to make paper patterns from which the glass for the practice panel will be cut to shape. The paper for patterns should be heavy "tag" paper. This is about the weight of file folders.

Take a piece of 14" x 16" pattern paper, lay carbon paper (carbon down) on it, place the cartoon face-up on top of the carbon paper, and hold this arrangement firm with thumbtacks (Fig. 6). Trace over all lines of the design, except the outside cartoon perimeter line. Number each piece before lifting both cartoon and carbon paper (Fig. 7).

Each pattern must represent the EXACT size of the piece of glass as it fits in the panel. This necessitates allowing space between each piece of glass for the heart of the lead. The space is approximately 1/16".

The pattern paper now shows the numbered pieces of the design and the inside perimeter line. Cut along the perimeter line with regular scissors. The lines of the design are cut with 3-bladed pattern shears that remove a 1/16" strip between pieces to allow for the heart of the lead. In place of pattern shears a knife with two blades set 1/16" apart may be used, or draw a double line 1/16" apart and cut along both lines with regular scissors.

Cutting patterns
using pattern shears
with right hand
beneath patterns for
better control.
Fig. 8

Cutting patterns
using utility knife.
Fig. 9

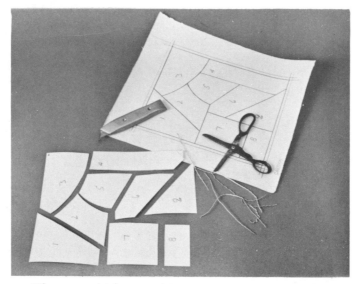

Glass cutting patterns.
Fig. 10

When using pattern shears cut with a series of short 1/2" strokes. The pattern paper should be held firmly in the left hand close to the blade of the shears. Pressure should continuously be applied to the paper so that it is fed into the jaws of the shears as they move along the line 1/2" at a time. Using short strokes allows you to keep moving your left hand so that you can feed the paper. It keeps the 1/16" strip from getting stuck between the two bottom blades, and it makes it easier to maneuver around curved shapes (Fig. 8). Sharper the curve, shorter the strokes.

A utility knife with two blades and a piece of lead or wood separating the blades will also cut out the required strip. They are less expensive, but require more effort to maintain a clean even 1/16" strip (Fig. 9).

Of course, if you'd rather not make any investment at first, simply draw your patterns with a double line ——— 1/16" apart and carefully trim the 1/16" strip away with ordinary household scissors.

After all the patterns are cut (Fig. 10) you are ready to cut the glass to shape. Choosing the colors of glass and the order in which to cut out the pieces is for you to decide. Following are some suggestions that may be of assistance as you proceed to cut your glass to shape.

Cutting away excess glass before
cutting to shape.
Fig. 11

Cutting difficult edge first.
Fig. 12

1. Make a test cut on each side of a piece
   of glass of the type you've chosen to
   determine which side is easiest to score
   and break. In general Blenko antique
   glass is scored on the smooth side and
   European on the slightly more textured
   side. Flashed glass, glass coated with
   a thin layer of color on only one side,
   is always scored on the non-flashed
   side. Cathedral and Opalescent are
   always cut on the smooth side.

2. Position the pattern on the glass and
   cut away any large excess of glass
   before cutting to shape (Fig. 11). This
   prevents an improper break from ruining
   a large piece of your favorite color
   glass.

3. When scoring along the edge of the
   pattern do not let the pattern slip. A
   slip of even 1/32" can cause the piece
   of glass to fit incorrectly when the
   piece is leaded into a panel.

4. It is often convenient to make the most
   difficult score first. If it fails to
   break correctly the pattern can be
   moved and the cut again attempted. In
   Fig. 12 the first score would be the
   concave one.

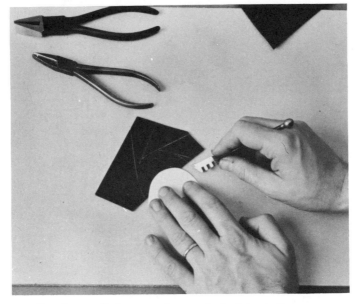

Series of tangent scores to cut
convex shape.
Fig. 13

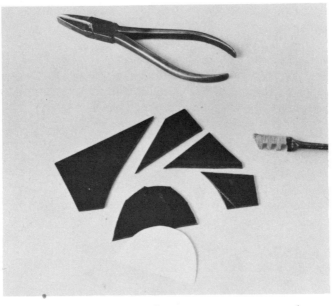

Convex shape cut but not yet grozed.
Fig. 14

5. If, after attempting to cut a piece to shape two or three times, it is not correct (this will happen at first), go on to another piece. Often a technique hit upon in cutting later pieces can be used to handle a difficult shape.

6. If you cut out a shape a couple of times but it fails to exactly be the shape of the pattern, stop, practice these pieces on scrap glass until successful, then again try the colored glass.

7. Excessive grozing leads to accidental breakage. It is easier to recut pieces that require grozing all around. Grozing can also become a crutch that hinders development of one's skill in cutting glass.

8. Convex curves are easier to obtain by use of a series of short tangent scores rather than a long, continuous curved score even though a ragged cut results that must be grozed (Figs. 13, 14).

9. If you make and break your cuts successfully and the piece still does not fit the pattern exactly, you must be moving the pattern while you are making your score. Hold it more firmly and make sure after each break to check that it has not slipped.

Breaking glass on edge of bench.
Fig. 15

10. When breaking straight lines it may help
    to lay the score 1/4" over the edge of
    the bench and, using your right hand to
    hold the glass on the bench, snap the
    glass off at the score by pressing down
    with the left hand on the extended
    part of the glass (Fig. 15).

Cartoon framed preparatory for
glazing.

Fig. 1

Lead vice.

Fig. 2

Chapter 3
Leading and Soldering

The next two tasks, leading (glazing) and soldering, will be covered in this chapter.

Before beginning to glaze the panel you need lead, a glazing knife, stopping knife, glazing nails, and a piece of 1/2" or 3/4" plywood two to three feet square unless you have a wooden work table.

Take your cartoon, place it on the work bench or plywood, and frame it on two adjacent sides, along the outside perimeter, with 1/2" x 1 1/2" x 18" sticks nailed through the cartoon into the work bench. When finished the two sticks form a right angle (Fig. 1). A left handed person may find it easier to place the board on the left side in Fig. 1 to the right side of the cartoon.

The lead, 1/2" flat for outside and 1/4" round for between pieces of glass, comes in 7' lengths that are limp and slightly twisted. Stretching the lead 3-4" makes it easier to handle and cut by straightening it and making it more rigid.

Stretch the lead by placing one end in a lead vice (Fig. 2) and pull the other end with pliers. As an alternative, two people with pliers can pull the lead. Other

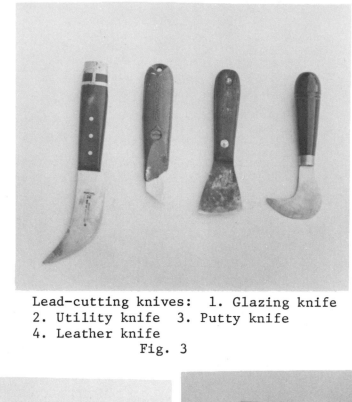

Lead-cutting knives: 1. Glazing knife
2. Utility knife   3. Putty knife
4. Leather knife
Fig. 3

Stopping knife.
Fig. 4

Horseshoe nails.
Fig. 5

methods are to stand on one end or jam it in the door and pull the other end with pliers.

To cut lead use a glazing knife or utility knife, sharpened putty knife, or leather knife (Fig. 3).

For cutting the smaller round leads you may want to try using a plier called a "DIA-GONAL CUTTER". It is designed for cutting wire, but works very well on some leads. With a little practice, you will be able to make very accurate cuts with less effort than is required with the knife.

A stopping knife (Fig.4) is used to help properly position both lead and glass. The stopping knife has a curved dull blade and a blob of lead is usually cast onto the end of the handle. Glazing knives also often have lead cast onto the handle.

Glazing nails are needed to hold the glass and lead in place as you assemble your panel (Fig.5). Horseshoe nails are approximately the right length and are advantageous as their sides are flat and easily positioned against the glass.

The first step in glazing is to take a strip of 1/2" flat lead and lay a piece against each framing board, butting the ends at the corner, and cut each strip off longer than the edge of the panel.

Hands holding lead
and glazing knife
preparatory to
cutting.
Fig. 7

Mitred lead
Fig. 8

Cartoon in frame with two outside
1/2" leads.
Fig. 9

Before this you may want to practice
cutting lead. Don't forget to stretch it
first. To cut the lead hold it firmly on
the work bench with the fingers of the left
hand, place the glazing knife close to the
fingers, and cut through the lead slowly.
Rock the knife slightly from left to right
as you cut unless the knife has a curved
blade, in which case rock the blade back
and forth. The rocking motion should be
VERY SLIGHT, as should be your pressing on
the lead. Light pressure with the slight
rocking motion will allow the blade to
slowly work its way through without
crushing the heart of the lead (Fig. 7).

The heart of crushed lead can be
straightened with some manipulation with
the stopping knife, but it is a time-
consuming task. Practice cutting until you
can cut a clean straight cut that does not
crush the heart. You will need to cut
leads at an angle (mitre), so practice that
also - the procedure is the same, slow and
gentle with a slight rocking motion (Fig. 8).

Position and cut your two framing 1/2"
flat leads (Fig. 9). Hold the framing leads
in place with glazing nails.

The first piece of glass (#8) should be
inserted between the leaves of the lead and
tapped into place with the "lead hammer" on
the end of your stopping or glazing knife.
The curved blade of the stopping knife can

Fig. 10

Piece #8 in place.

Fig. 11

Lead cut short and positioned
along top of piece #8.

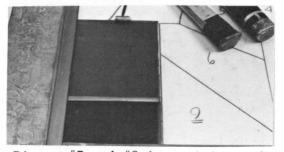

Fig. 12

Pieces #7 and #8 in position and
separated by single horizontal
lead.

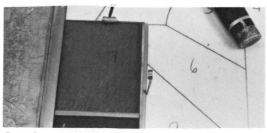

Fig. 13

Lead cut short and in position
along vertical edge of pieces
#7 and #8.

be inserted under the glass to lift it over the lower leaf of the lead. When properly in place it will feel solid when you tap and fit it within the cartoon line of piece #8 (Fig. 10).

Next, cut a piece of 1/4" round lead to fit between piece #8 and #7, the next piece to be put into place. This lead should butt against the outside lead and be approximately 1/16" short of the inside edge of piece #8 (Fig. 11). Short cutting the lead is to allow for the overlap of the leaf from the vertical lead along piece #7 and #8 that separates it from #9 and #6. Use the blade of the stopping knife to press the heart of the lead firmly against piece #8.

Position piece #7, tap it into the lead, and put a single nail along the top edge of #7 to hold the two pieces of glass and lead (Fig. 12). In Fig. 12 a short piece of scrap lead is placed between the glazing nail and glass to prevent chipping of the glass. This is generally used with thin glass or flashed glass which easily chips. Cut a piece of 1/4" lead to fit along the right hand edges of #7 and #8; butt it against the perimeter lead and stop 1/16" before the top edge of piece #7 (Fig. 13).

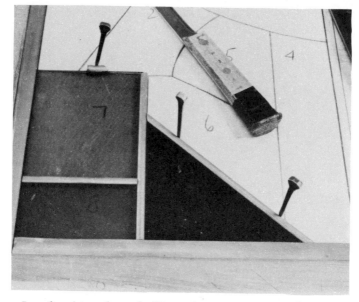

Lead mitred and fit along edge of #9.
Fig. 14

Sharpening glazing knife.
Fig. 15

Now insert piece #9, tap it into place.
Hold piece #9 in place with a nail while
you cut a piece of 1/4" lead to fit the
edge of #9. Mitre the ends so that they
butt flat to the leads they touch (Fig. 14).

Sharpening Your Glazing Knife

Since you are cutting lead which, though
soft, is a metal, your knife will get dull
quickly. You must have a sharpening stone
that is not too coarse. Use light oil on
the stone to keep it clean. Place the
cutting edge on the stone and raise the
knife handle about 1" from the surface of
the stone (approximately 15°). Push the
knife forward along the stone as though
trying to shave off a thin layer of stone.
Keep the knife at the same angle to the
stone throughout the stroke. Pick blade up
and repeat forward stroke, then turn blade
over and do the other side (Fig. 15).

You will need to do this frequently and,
if it is done properly, only two to four
strokes are needed to restore the sharpness
to the blade.

Fig. 16

Piece #1 in position with lead.

Fig. 17

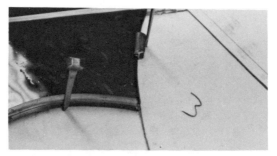

Piece #2 in position with lead.

Fig. 18

Lead in position along #5 and #6.

Fig. 19

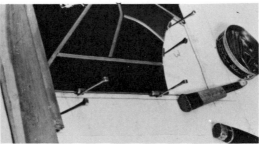

Piece #4 in place.

Put #6 in place and use nails to hold it
while you cut a piece of lead to fit
between pieces [#7, #6] and [#1, #2, #5].
Cut it off 1/16" short of the edge of #6.
Cut the lead so that it is parallel to the
right hand edge of #6. Now place #1 into
leads and tap into place. Use a nail to
hold #1. Cut a lead to run between pieces
#1 and #2. The piece #1 is one of the top
pieces of the panel. When you cut your
lead cut it 1/4" short of the top edge of
the glass. This is so that the 1/2"
perimeter lead will have room to fit over
the glass and will butt up against the 1/4"
lead (Fig. 16). Tap #2 into place; use a
nail to hold it. Cut a lead to fit between
#2 and #5. Cut it 1/16" short of the top
edge of #2 (Fig. 17).

Make sure that the lead closely follows
the curve of the glass. Tap #5 into place;
hold it with a nail. Cut a lead to fit
between [#5, #6] and #4. Cut it 1/16"
short of the top edge of #5 (Fig. 18).
Tap #4 into place, Make sure that it
doesn't extend beyond the inside perimeter
line (Fig. 19). Use nails to hold it in
place.

Cut a lead to fit between [#2, #5, #4]
and #3. Cut the end 1/4" short of the right
hand edge of #4 so that the 1/2" perimeter
lead will have room to overlap the glass
and butt against the end of the 1/4" lead.

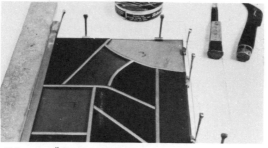

Fig. 20

Piece #3 in place.

Fig. 21

Fitting outside vertical lead.

Fig. 22

Outside horizontal lead in place.

Fig. 23

Patch in place to fill space
between leads.

Tap #3 into place making sure that it does not extend beyond the inside perimeter line. Use nails to hold (Fig. 20).

You are now ready to put your 1/2" outside perimeter lead onto the remaining two edges of your panel.

Cut a piece of 1/2" lead to fit along the right side of your panel. Butt it to the bottom 1/2" lead and cut it 1/4" short of the top edge of your panel. Use your stopping knife to push the lead right to the edge of the glass. The outside perimeter full size line should be even with the outside edge of the lead (Fig. 21).

Now, place a piece of 1/2" lead on the top edge of your panel. Cut it off even with the outside edge of the right side lead. Use nails to hold the panel together (Fig. 22).

Soldering

Where two leads butt each other you need to solder them together. If there are any spaces between the end of one lead and the side of the intersecting lead, you must cut a small scrap of lead to form a patch or bridge for the solder to stick to (Fig. 23).

Scratched lead joint.
Fig. 24

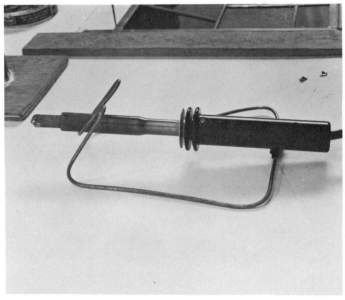

Soldering iron.
Fig. 25

At each intersection or joint where
solder is to be applied, clean the lead so
that the solder will stick. Use a small
wire brush or your knife to scratch up the
surface of the lead at each joint (Fig. 24).

Apply a small amount of OLEIC ACID FLUX
to each joint. Flux is necessary, since
without it the solder will not stick to the
lead.

Soldering Iron

An electric soldering iron of 80 to 200
watts is essential for soldering your
panel (Fig. 25). A gun-type will not work.

When your soldering iron has heated up
sufficiently to readily melt solder, then
you may begin soldering the joints. Make
sure you have put flux on all joints. If
the iron is too hot it will burn the lead
away. Test it first on scrap lead. To
keep your iron heating properly you should
keep the tip clean and smoothly tinned.

Preparing to solder
joint.
Fig. 26

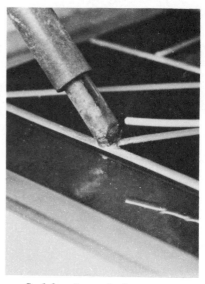

Soldering joint.

Fig. 27

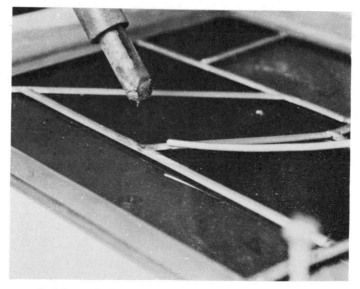

Soldered joint.
Fig. 28

To Tin an Iron

File the copper tip to the desired
shape, smooth so that there are no pitted
parts or caked oxidation. Now heat the
soldering iron. Take a cake of rosin,
purchased at a violin store, and insert the
tip of the soldering iron into the rosin.
Now coat the tip with solder and wipe off
the excess with a rag. The soldering iron
is now tinned and ready for use. Re-tin
the soldering iron whenever the tip gets
pitted. Keep it clean during use by wiping
it frequently with a rag or a damp sponge.

Use solid-core 50/50 or 60/40 tin-lead
solder in 1/8" wire form.

Lay the wire solder along the joint of
two pieces of lead and, with the flat edge
of the heated soldering iron, press down on
the wire solder until the solder melts and
flows smoothly across the joint. Lift the
iron straight up off the joint (Figs. 26,
27, 28).

If you try to smear the solder around
you will get an ugly rough joint. You need
practice with the soldering iron to
determine how long to hold the iron on the
joint so that it heats up the lead
sufficiently, but does not burn it.

Improperly soldered
joint.
Fig. 29

Soldered perimeter
leads.
Fig. 30

Completely soldered panel.
Fig. 31

If your solder "peaks" like meringue,
then your iron is probably not hot enough,
or you have no flux on your joint (Fig. 29).

Solder all the joints on your panel.
Don't forget the four corners (Fig. 30).
If you do burn a lead, cut a small patch to
fill the hole and solder over it. Don't
forget the flux.

Now turn your panel over and solder the
joints on the other side.

The two long perimeter leads can now
be trimmed flush at the corners of the
panel. The completely soldered and
trimmed panel should look like Fig. 31.

Cementing tools.

Fig. 1

Chapter 4
Cementing Your Panel

To make your panel water-tight and
strong, you must cement it. Cementing also
cleans the glass and lead and darkens the
leads and soldered joints so that they do
not reflect light.

Mix your own cement from stratch:

> 4 parts Whiting
> 2 parts Plaster of Paris
> 1 1/2 parts Turpentine
> 1 part Boiled Linseed Oil
> 1/2 part Portland Cement
> Sprinkle powdered Lampblack to color

Mix to a thick mud, add whiting to
thicken or turpentine to thin.

Or, you can buy some old-fashioned
putty (not glazing compound). To the
putty you add:

> Turpentine to thin
> Portland Cement (handful)
> Lampblack to color

Mix to thick mud, add whiting to thicken
or turpentine to thin.

Lay out some newspaper on your bench and
put on old clothes. You will need two
scrub brushes, a rag, and a pointed stick
the size of a pencil (Fig. 1).

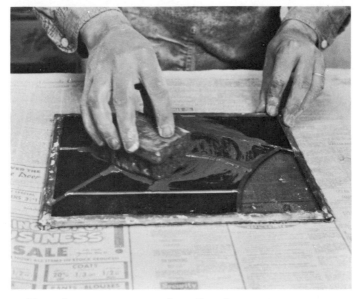

Forcing cement under lead grooves.
Fig. 2

Spreading whiting.
Fig. 3

Use one scrub brush to rub cement over one side of panel, force cement under all the grooves (Fig. 2).

Sprinkle a handful of whiting over the panel and spread it over the surface with a rag. Whiting helps dry the cement (Fig. 3).

Trimming cement even with edge of leads.

Fig. 4

Scrubbing panel clean.

Fig. 5

Excess cement will be piled around each lead. Hold the stick and use it to cut the cement off even with the edge of the lead (Fig. 4).

Sprinkle another handful of whiting and scrub panel clean with the other brush (Fig. 5). Whiting also helps clean grease from the glass. Repeat process on second side.

The longer you scrub, the darker the solder and lead will become.

When both sides are clean lay panel flat for 8-12 hours. Then use the stick to clean off any cement which has oozed out of the leads. Panel should lay flat for at least 36 hours before being installed.

Irregular shaped
hangings.
Fig. 1

Lampshade.
Fig. 2

Rolls of copper foil.
Fig. 3

Chapter 5
Copper Foil Technique

An alternate method of assembling your
glass pieces is to use copper foil and
solder in place of the lead.

This method is best for irregular-
shaped hangings (Fig. 1) or when the
individual pieces of glass are so small
that the lead between them would look overly
bulky or cover them entirely.

Make a drawing and patterns and cut out
your glass exactly as in Chapters 1 and 2.
Take each piece of glass and wrap the
edge with a strip of copper foil. Use
adhesive-backed copper foil which comes on
a 1/4" width 36 yard roll (Fig. 3).

Copper foil is used in making lampshades
as it is stronger than lead came and will
support the weight of the glass (Fig. 2).

Glass edge centered
on foil.
Fig. 4

Cutting foil to
correct length.
Fig. 5

Take the first piece of glass and place it's edge in the middle of a strip of copper. Wrap the strip around the entire edge of the piece being careful to keep the glass in the middle of the foil so that an equal amount of foil shows on both sides of the glass (Fig. 4). Overlap the ends of foil 1/4" and cut off excess (Fig. 5).

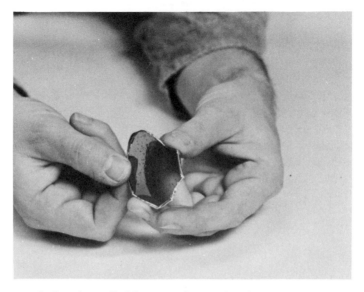

Crimping foil to edge of glass.
Fig. 6

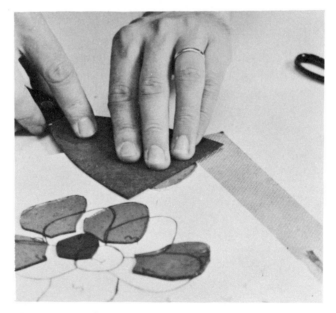

Pressing foil tight to glass.
Fig. 7

Now crimp the foil around the edge of
the glass (Fig. 6) and, laying the piece on
a flat surface, press foil tight to the
glass with the blade of a putty knife
(Fig. 7).

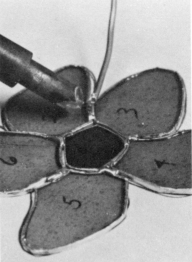

Foiled pieces in
position on drawing.
Fig. 8

Tacking pieces
together with solder.
Fig. 9

Lay the pieces down on your drawing in their proper order (Fig. 8).

Now apply flux. Fluxes are available which can easily be sprayed from a spray bottle. Some of these are toxic and should be avoided, especially the acid types. All fluxes should be used outdoors or with a fan running. The safest that I have found so far is called LA-CO regular flux.

When flux is on all the copper take the soldering iron and solder several of the joints where pieces of glass come together so that it will not slip apart when you are working on it (Fig. 9). Remove your drawing if you plan to use it again.

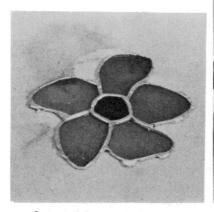

One side completely
soldered.
Fig. 10

Melting excess
solder off edge.
Fig. 11

Wear glasses when soldering copperfoil.

With a hot iron flow solder over all the copper on one side, flop the design over and do the same (Fig. 10). Don't forget flux.

Do not worry if blobs of solder flow off the edge of the design, they will be useful later.

When the solder has cooled sufficiently, pick the design up and, holding it at arms length, use the iron to melt the excess blobs of solder from the edge of the design, at the same time coating the copper around the edge of the design (Fig. 11).

Soldering wire loop.
Fig. 12

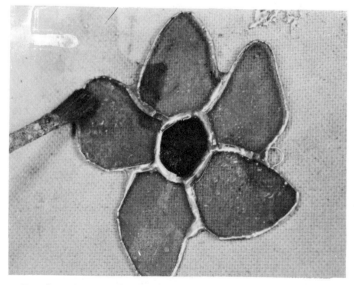

Darkening solder.
Fig. 13

No copper should be showing and the pieces of glass are firmly held together

At a strong point or two, solder a wire loop or jump ring to hang the design (Fig. 12).

To darken the solder or give it an antique look use copper sulfate ($CuSO_4$) crystals dissolved in hot water. You can get anywhere from a grey to black to copper color, depending on how strong a solution of $CuSO_4$ you make (Fig. 13).

Brush the copper sulfate solution over the soldered surfaces. Wash the design with detergent and a sponge. Do not use the sponge for anything else as the $CuSO_4$ is poison. Do not wipe the design dry. Let it drain on paper towels or newspaper.

Glossary

Aciding
Process of etching the thin layer of
color off the surface of flash glass,
in order to allow the base color to
show through. For example, on flashed
ruby on white; to allow portions of
white to show through the ruby flash,
mask the parts you wish to remain ruby,
using bees wax or asphaltum varnish,
immerse the piece in hydrofluoric acid
or dab acid on the exposed ruby. The
acid will slowly eat away the ruby
leaving the white base color exposed.
See sandblasting for an alternate
etching method.

Antique Glass
The commercial term applied to glass
made by the ancient hand-blown method.
The glass blower blows a large bubble or
cylinder of glass, which is then cut
open and flattened into a small sheet
containing seeds and reams and varying
in thickness from 1/16" to 1/4" within
the same sheet. Antique glass is very
transparent and its irregularity and
spontaneity of texture make it very
beautiful and ideally suited for use in
leaded glass windows.

Badger Blender
A flat long badger-haired brush used
to spread a matt of glass paint evenly
over the surface of a piece of glass.

Banding
    Soldering copper wires to the inside
surface of a leaded panel, so that it
can be fastened to its support bars by
twisting the wires around the bars
during installation.

Blenko Antique
    Hand-blown glass made by Blenko Glass
Co., Milton, West Virginia

Cartoon
    Full-size drawing of window showing all
the details of leading and painting.

Cathedral Glass
    The commercial name applied to glass
which is machine made. It is rolled
out into large sheets having various
lumpy textures rolled onto one surface.
It is usually very even in thickness
throughout the sheet. It is made in
numerous colors and textures and, since
it is less expensive than Antique, is a
good choice for first projects.

Cementing
    Forcing putty into the grooves of lead
to make a leaded window waterproof and
strong. This process also cleans the
glass and darkens the leads.

Cutline
    A tracing of the cartoon showing only
the outline of the separate pieces of
glass. It is used for glazing the
panel and by the English, who do not
cut out patterns, but rather place the
piece of glass on top of the cut line

and try to follow the outline of the
piece with their cutter. They become
quite accurate at cutting just
inside the line, thereby allowing for
the heart of the lead. Today a light-
box is used beneath the cutline, but for
dark pieces a pattern must still be made.

Dalle-de-verre
The French name for slab glass. Cast
pieces 1" x 8" x 12" set in concrete or
epoxy to make windows.

Easel
Large piece of plate glass set upright
in front of a window. As pieces of
stained glass are cut to shape they can
be stuck up on the easel with bees wax
or plasticene. Seen with daylight
passing through them the colors of the
pieces can be judged as pleasing or
not. The pieces can again be stuck up
in place on the easel when it comes
time to apply paint.

Flash Glass
Glass with a thin layer of colored
glass fused onto the thicker base
color, which is usually white, such as
flashed ruby on white. Flash glass
allows the use of certain intense colors
which, if they were the full thickness
of the glass, would be so dark as to
appear black. It also allows for rapid
change in shading from light to dark, or

swirls and streaks of one or more colors.
It also can be etched. (See aciding and
sandblasting.)

Flux
A substance applied to the leads to clean
them and keep them from oxidizing while
being soldered. The solder will not flow
smoothly or stick without flux. In
stained glass work Oleic acid is most
commonly used.

Frying
Tiny pinholes which develop in the paint
while it is being fired. Usually from
too much gum arabic used in mixing paint,
or from trying to paint over tracing
before firing.

Full-size line
Herein called the outside perimeter line.

Glass-size line
Herein called the inside perimeter line.

Glazing
The act of assembling pieces of glass and
lead came together to form a window.

Glazing knife
Knife used to cut lead came when glazing
a panel. The cutting edge can be
straight or curved to aid in the rocking
motion used in cutting through the lead.

Glazing nails
Nails used to hold glass and lead in
position as the glazier puts the panel
together piece by piece. In this book
horseshoe nails are used.

Grissaille
(Glass paint) The French name for the
black or brown paint used to add
details to leaded glass windows. It is
made from metallic oxides and powdered
glass so that when fired in a kiln it
becomes part of the surface of the
glass. It is applied opaque for line
detail or as a matt which is stippled
and scratched away to produce shadow
effects. Also the name for a type of
window using mostly clear or pale glass
with designs painted in black.

Groze
To bite or chip unwanted bits from the
edge of a piece of glass using a
grozing plier.

Grozing iron
In ancient times a flat iron bar with
various size notches in its edge was
used as an aid in shaping glass. In
modern times it is largely replaced by
the more efficient nipper and grozing
pliers.

Grozing plier
  Flat-nosed plier with the temper
  removed from the steel and the edges of
  the jaws filed round.

Gum Arabic
  A sticky substance, a small amount of
  which is mixed into glass paint to
  help it stick to the glass.

Heart
  Refers to the center post of the lead
  came. The cross bar of the "H" section.

Lampblack
  A colorant for paints and grout. Used
  to darken cement for leaded glass.

Lathekin
  A small, flat tool made of hard wood or
  bone used to open or manipulate lead
  came. Similar in use to a stopping
  knife. Teflon makes the best lead opener.

Lead cames
  (calmes, calms, kamz) Strips of lead used
  between pieces of stained glass to hold
  them together as a window. They are cast
  or extruded to the shape of small I-beams
  varying in size from 1/8" to 1" or more.
  When seen in cross-section, normal lead
  came looks like an "H". Certain lead
  seen in section looks like a "U", it is
  sometimes used to wrap around the outside edge of panels.

Leaded glass
Windows or panels made of pieces of
glass, usually colored, held together
with grooved strips of lead.

Leading
See glazing or lead cames

Lead vise
A mechanism which holds one end of lead
securely while glazier pulls on the
other end with pliers. A jam cleat
from a boat is an ideal lead vise.

Leaf
Refers to the part of the lead came
which fits over the edge of the glass.
The uprights in the "H" section.

Nippers
Special pliers used an as aid in
cutting glass.

Opalescent Glass
The commercial name given to a variety
of glass having a semi-opaque coloring
which makes it less transparent than
Cathedral or Antique glass. It is
machine rolled like Cathedral. It
came into use in USA in the 19th century
and was used extensively in windows and
lampshades.

Patterns
Heavy paper templates used to guide
cutter. They are made from a tracing of
the cutline. Approximately a 1/16"
strip of paper is cut from between each
pattern to allow for the heart of the
lead. This makes each pattern exactly
the size of the piece of glass to be
cut.

Pattern shears
Special scissors having two blades on the
bottom and one on the top which allows
it to cut out a strip of paper the exact
width of the top blade. They are used in
cutting out patterns as they allow space
between each pattern for the heart of the
lead.

Plating
Leading a piece of glass on top of another
to change its color. The two pieces can
be sandwiched together and leaded into
the panel as one piece, or the second
piece may be leaded on top of the first
when the panel has been completed.

Quarries
Diamonds or rectangles of glass, usually
leaded together in a simple trellis or
lattice design.

Reamy
Refers to glass that has waves or
streaks.

Sandblasting
Method used for etching the thin layer of
color off the surface of the flash glass
in order to allow the base color to show
through. Portions of the flash which
are to remain are masked with two layers
of masking tape, then the glass is
subjected to a pressurized spray of fine
sand which abrades away the unmasked
flash. (See Aciding for the traditional
method of etching flashed glass.)

Seeds
The tiny bubbles which add sparkle to
certain types of glass.

Silver stain
A mixture using silver salts which,
when fired onto the surface of glass,
results in various shades of yellow,
permanently staining the glass. Hence
the name "stained glass." The action of
silver stain was not discovered until
the 14th century.

Solder
A combination of tin and lead which
melts at a lower temperature than lead
and is used to hold two pieces of lead
together. It is made in various
percentages of tin and lead. 40%-60%
tin is best for leaded glass work, it
will be sold as 40/60 or 50/50 or
60/40 and comes in 1/8" wide wire in
one pound rolls.

Soldering
>Using a hot iron to melt solder and
make it stick to two intersecting leads
to hold them together.

Stained glass
>A leaded glass window or panel having the
addition of painting and staining, using
grissalle and silver stain. In popular
usage leaded glass and stained glass are
used interchangeably.

Stippling
>Method used to brush away the matt of
glass paint to let light show through to
produce shadow effects. A stippling
brush has all the hairs the same length
and is usually made of badger. The ends
of the hairs are used to poke tiny holes
in the matt of paint.

Stopping knife
>A flat dull-bladed knife with the end
usually bent upwards 30°-40°. Often
made from an oyster knife. Usually a
blob of lead is cast onto the end of
the handle to be used as a hammer to tap
glass snugly into place and to drive in
glazing nails.

Striations
>Surface marks on some Antique glass,
they look like scratches and give the
glass a crystalline look.

Support bars
    Iron bars with ends embedded in frame to
    which the leaded panel is tied for
    support by means of copper wires. (See
    banding.)

Tinning
    Coating the copper tip of soldering
    iron with solder. Tip is shaped and
    smoothed with a file then heated and
    dipped into some rosin and then coated
    with solder. This cleans it and allows
    it to readily melt the solder.

Whiting
    Powdered calcium carbonate - chalk.

Bibliography

Theory:

1. "Stained Glass: Art or Anti-Art",
   John Piper. Studio Vista/Reinhold
   Art Paperback, 1968.

2. "The Jerusalem Windows of Marc
   Chagall", Jean Leymarie. George
   Braziller, New York, 1967.

3. "English Stained Glass", John Baker
   and Alfred Lammer. Henry N. Abrams,
   Inc., New York.

4. "Stained Glass, An Architectural Art",
   Robert Sowers. Universe Books,
   Inc., 381 Park Avenue South, New York,
   1965.

5. "The Language of Stained Glass",
   Robert Sowers, Timber Press, Forest
   Grove, Oregon, 1981.

6. "New Glass", Otto Rigan and Charles
   Frizzell, Ballantine Books, New York,
   1976.

7. "Architectural Stained Glass", Edited
   by Brian Clarke, Architectural Record
   Books/McGraw-Hill Book Co., New York,
   1979.

8. "Licht Glas Farbe", Oidtmann
   Studio/Verlag M. Brimberg, Aachen,
   West Germany, 1982.

Bibliography

Technique:

1. "Stained Glass", Lawrence Lee.
Oxford Paperbacks, Oxford University
Press, 1967.

2. "Stained Glass: History, Technology,
and Practice", E. Liddal Armitage.
Charles T. Branford Co., Newton 59,
Massachusetts, 1959.

3. "Technique of Stained Glass", Patrick
Reyntiens Watson-Guptill Publications,
New York, 1967.

4. "Making Stained Glass", Robert & Gertrude
Metcalf, McGraw-Hill Book Co., New York,
1972.

5. "Stained Glass Craft", J. Divine. F. Warne
& Co., 1940, reprinted by Dover Publications
1972.

6. "Working with Stained Glass", Jean Jacques
Duval, Thomas Y. Crowell Co., New York,
1972.

7. "The Art of Painting on Glass", Albinus
Elskus, Charles Scribner's Sons, New
York, 1980

"Next best thing to an apprenticeship."
— Diana Sloat, The Next Whole Earth Catalog

STAINED GLASS PRIMER, THE BASIC SKILLS

ステンドグラス入門　基本技術

by
ピーター　モリカ著　PETER MOLLICA

edited by
ノーム　フォーゲル編集　NORM FOGEL

写真技術　photography by
チャールズ　フリッツェル　CHARLES FRIZZELL

translation by
翻訳者　笹川英資　EISUKE SASAGAWA

第一巻：基礎技術　ケイムを使ったステンドグラス作業の技術、道具そしてコッパーフォイルの使い方が簡潔に指図され、わかりやすく説明してあります。

初心者用テキストブックとして、世界中の学校で使われています。

第一巻を1971年に発行、今回第十八巻目を出版。
140,000 冊売上突破。

mollica stained glass press

モリカ　ステンドグラス出版社

ISBN 0-9601306-4-0